Social Anxiety and Shyness Ultimate Guide:

Techniques to Overcome Stress, Achieve Self-Esteem, and Succeed as an Introvert

LISA KIMBERLY

Copyright © 2015 Lisa Kimberly

Simultaneously published in United States of America, the UK, India, Germany, France, Italy, Canada, Japan, Spain, and Brazil.

All right reserved. No part of this book may be reproduced in any form of by any other electronic or mechanical means – except in the case of brief quotations embodies in articles or reviews –without written permission from its author.

Social Anxiety and Shyness Ultimate Guide has provided the most accurate information possible. Many of the techniques used in this book are from personal experiences. The author shall not be held liable for any damages resulting from use of this book.

All rights reserved.

ISBN: 1514310848
ISBN-13: 978-1514310847

FREE GIFT

Thank you for your purchase of my Social Anxiety and Shyness Ultimate Guide, as an extra bonus I want to give you a free gift. This is a FULL copy of my book Victory: How to Achieve Any Goal.

==>> http://lisakimberly.com/victory

This book is going to teach you a lot of exercises and techniques for overcoming your social anxiety. In Victory, I teach you how to build a plan for achieving a goal. How to take those exact tips and techniques and use them to change your life.

CONTENTS

Introduction · I

PART I: Exploring Shyness and Social Anxiety

1 Are you an Introvert? · 3
2 What is Social Anxiety? · 7
3 Social Anxiety, Self-Esteem and Stress · 10

PART II: Overcoming Social Anxiety and Shyness

4 Overcoming the Stress of Social Anxiety · 15
5 Improving Your Self-Esteem · 19
6 Taking Charge of Your Life · 22

PART III: Succeeding as an Introvert

7 Being an Introvert in an Extroverted World · 27
8 Building Confidence · 30
9 Introverts in the Workplace · 34
10 Introvert Icons · 37

Conclusion · 40

INTRODUCTION

My parents came into my room to talk to me.

"We think something's wrong with you. Why don't you have any friends. We found a really great therapist."

Those magic words started my own journey dealing with social anxiety and rejection for being an introvert.

My parents thought that there was something wrong with me. Like I had a disease.

Maybe it was contagious and all of their children would end up friendless and alone.

It's so scary when your parents think your brain is broken. You don't know what to do.

I didn't have zero friends.

I just had a few friends and I enjoyed my own company.

Social anxiety is stressful but it can also be overcome.

This book is to show you that you're not alone.

That there is nothing wrong with being introverted.

This is the book that I wish my parents had given me when I was sixteen instead of trying to fix me.

You can learn to build your confidence, overcome social anxiety and survive in an extroverts world.

There is nothing wrong with you.

You are an amazing person and by the end of this book you are going to release that amazing into the world with confidence!

Your social anxiety is going to melt away and your are going to find the same ability to express yourself in public that I have!

PART 1
EXPLORING SHYNESS AND SOCIAL ANXIETY

LISA KIMBERLY

1 ARE YOU AN INTROVERT?

"Aren't you having fun?" "Why don't you talk more?" "Are you just shy?" If you're an introvert, chances are good you have heard these questions a great many times. This book is for you!

Introversion and *introvert* are words you've probably heard. When you've heard them, it's likely been in a negative context. In our extrovert-dominated world, introverts definitely come up against a lot of misconceptions. You might suffer from social anxiety, and be frustrated with your shyness. Did you know, though, that introverts actually have quite a few advantages over extroverts? It's true!

In this book, we will first explore the concepts of introversion, shyness, and social anxiety. After that, we will give you real and effective tools you can use to truly empower yourself, and ensure that you live life to its fullest as the brilliant and dynamic introvert you are!

By the time you finish reading this book, you will no longer feel hindered by your shyness or social anxiety. You will feel empowered and no longer be hampered by social anxiety, and you will realize that you can harness your shyness and introversion in positive ways. Being an introvert can actually be an advantage. This book will show you how!

If you're an introvert (like we are), you are probably sick of people constantly accusing you of being too shy. Most people equate being an introvert with shyness and quietness, and a general tendency to be reserved.

It is true that we introverts often end up *seeming* shy and quiet to many people (especially extroverts). But it is also true that among the people we feel comfortable with, such as close friends and family, we can be just as gregarious and talkative as extroverts. We have at least as much knowledge, and as many ideas, as extroverts have. We have a lot within us to contribute to our world and society.

It is generally thought that we are outnumbered by extroverts by approximately three to one. Unfortunately, the fact that there are so many more extroverts than introverts in the world has led to our widespread marginalization and stigmatization. There are many misconceptions about us, and there is a definite tendency in Western cultures to label and rather dismiss us. This often makes it quite difficult for us to fully participate in many different vital areas of society, such as school and the workplace. Thankfully, this book will give you the tools you need to show the world all of your talents and substantial gifts! We are deep thinkers. This gives us a distinct advantage over extroverts—if we know how to harness all the power of our intelligence!

Introversion and extroversion are measured on a continuum. The means that there is really no such thing as a person who is absolutely 100% extrovert or introvert. However, most people have personalities that are dominated mostly by either extroverted or introverted characteristics, and many people are extremely strongly either introvert or extrovert.

You are probably asking how to effectively differentiate between us and extroverts. To get you started, here are some examples of differences that generally exist:

- We generally need more time alone. We use this time by ourselves to "recharge" and gain new energy. We tend to generally be on the sensitive side, and can become over-stimulated much more easily than extroverts. Not being able to take breaks from social interaction can emotionally drain us. Extroverts, on the other hand, actually re-energize through social interaction, and usually hate being alone.
- We will most often think first and act later. We are less likely to be attracted to risk-taking than extroverts. Extroverts have a tendency towards acting first and thinking later.
- We tend to have a very strong degree of self-awareness. We have extensive knowledge of our own feelings and thoughts, and strong introspective abilities. Extroverts tend to be much weaker in this area.
- We are excellent observers and listeners, while extroverts tend to spend much more time talking and acting than watching and listening.
- We tend to hate engaging in small talk. We much prefer having deep conversations about ideas.
- We are better at abstract thinking, and tend to be deep thinkers.
- We tend to be good at learning by observation.

As we mentioned earlier, the majority of people in the world are extroverts. So, extroversion tends to be favored and seen as the "norm". This is especially the case in Western cultures, where extroversion in general, in pretty much every part of life, is seen as most desirable. These circumstances tend to be very difficult for us to deal with. The more introverted we are, the more difficult this tends to be. It is hard to be a well-adjusted, confident person who is constantly besieged with insinuations that you are somehow abnormal and should change to become more of an extrovert.

Unfortunately, extroverts grow up in a culture that reinforces their idea that the way they are always the best way to be, and are usually not made to value different perspectives on the matter. As a result, extroverted people tend to not make much of an effort to understand us and recognize that the introverted personality is just as valid as the extroverted personality. When we have to face this reality every day of our lives, it is easy to develop an inferiority complex. It is easy to start believing that we are lacking in some way.

We tend to seek to avoid confrontation. That combined with a confidence level that has been constantly under attack by an extroverted world often makes it very difficult for us to stand up for ourselves.

As an introvert, you should learn more about your personality and what an introvert's emotional needs are. Do not let anyone dismiss the validity of your needs, your personality, and your unique nature. Doing so will help increase your confidence. It will make you more aware of the necessity of standing up for yourself and asserting yourself. Gaining the confidence you deserve is one of the most important steps you can take in order to ensure you can reach your potential, and live your life to its fullest.

So, what do you think? Are you an introvert? If you're still not sure, take this quick test! It will tell you whether or not it is likely that you an introvert. For each question, choose one answer. At the end of the test, you will find a scoring key. Have fun!

1. After a long day at work with lots of meetings, what would you most enjoy as a way to unwind?
    a) Going to the pub or to a fun get-together with co-workers.
    b) Spending some quiet time at home alone, watching a great movie and eating your favorite food.

2. Which of these occupations would you prefer?
    a) Professional public speaker
    b) Novelist

3. Would you describe yourself as outgoing?
    a) Yes
    b) No, or not usually.

4. You are at a party. What are you most likely to be doing?
   a) Freely moving from group to group, effortlessly taking part in small talk and introductions.
   b) Talking with one or two close friends.

5. How often do you feel the need to be alone?
   a) Rarely, or never.
   b) I frequently feel the need to be alone, especially after spending a lot of time in any kind of social situation.

6. Which of these do you usually prefer?
   a) Fun and lively small talk.
   b) A deep or philosophical conversation.

The more a) answers you chose, the more extroverted you are. The more b) answers you chose, the more introverted you are. Therefore, if the majority of your answers were b) selections, then it's time to celebrate, because you are probably an introvert, and you are about to learn about how to show the world how wonderful you really are!

2 WHAT IS SOCIAL ANXIETY?

Do you tend to feel nervous before or during social situations of any kind? How severe is this anxiety? Have other people noticed it? As you might have guessed, social anxiety is anxiety or fear that arises with regard to present or future social situations.

People who have social anxiety generally fear that they will embarrass themselves. They fear that they will make people think badly of them in some way, without a rational reason. We introverts can find social situations emotionally draining when we do not have ample chances for a break to recharge, and this can affect thinking and the processing of emotions. So, social anxiety is generally more likely to be experienced by us.

People who experience a level of social anxiety may be shy, and certainly probably give the impression of being shy. But social anxiety cannot be dismissed simply as shyness. Shyness is a very general and encompassing term. It is used so casually and broadly that it is often used as a way to minimize or dismiss something more serious.

When social anxiety is so severe as to significantly interfere in living day to day life as you would wish to live it otherwise, there is a possibility of the presence of Social Anxiety Disorder. Social Anxiety Disorder is a psychiatric anxiety disorder in which people have an intense and quite overwhelming fear of being watched and judged by others. People with this disorder always tend to assume that they will be judged negatively and severely. They think this even when there is no reason why this should be the case.

Those of us suffering from Social Anxiety Disorder might have a panic attack either during a social situation. Or this panic attack might take place even substantially before a social situation will actually take place. Panic attacks can include a racing heart, rapid and difficult breathing, chest pains, feeling disoriented or weak, experiencing a feeling of extreme fear, numbness or a tingling sensation in the fingers and hands, unexplained sweating, chills, and a strong feeling of powerlessness. This can lead people with this disorder to seek to simply avoid any kind of social situation completely. This can clearly interfere with many different facets of life. These facets of life can include especially vital ones, like school and work.

Social Anxiety Disorder is very distressing. This is especially true as many people with this disorder actually rationally acknowledge that their fears are baseless, but find it almost impossible to dismiss or overcome them. People who have Social Anxiety Disorder usually experience anxiety in relation to a wide variety of different situations. These can include everyday situations. Examples can include talking on the phone, asking people questions, and even eating in front of other people.

Social Anxiety Disorder is the third most prevalent mental disorder, and the second most prevalent anxiety disorder in the United States. It is believed that there are over 19 million people in the United States who have this disorder. Social Anxiety is found more often in women than in men.

Social Anxiety Disorder is diagnosed primarily by psychiatrists and psychologists. Cognitive behavioral therapy (CBT) and/or medication may be used in the treatment of this disorder. Cognitive behavioral therapy is the most popular method of treatment. It is also common to combine cognitive behavioral therapy with the use of medication. Examples of other helpful approaches are specialized counseling with the goal of strengthening the patient's social skills and self-esteem, and the learning of special relaxation techniques. Breathing techniques are usually included here.

In their discussions about Social Anxiety Disorder, experts generally split social situations into two types: performance situations, and interpersonal interactions. Examples of performance situations include public speaking, walking into a room that is already full of people, performing on a stage (acting in a play, singing, or playing a musical instrument, for example), and taking part in meetings. Examples of interpersonal interactions include a job interview, putting forth an opinion, meeting new people, conversation, attending social functions like dinners and parties, and taking part in group work (at school or at work).

Based on what you have read, do you think you might have social anxiety to some degree, or perhaps even Social Anxiety Disorder? Do you experience anxiety and fear during or before social situations? How intense is that fear? Does it interfere with your life? If it does, how severely does it interfere with your life? If you think you might have social anxiety, and especially if you think you might have Social Anxiety Disorder, you owe it yourself to take action.

If you think you might have Social Anxiety Disorder, it is advisable to see a doctor or psychologist, as the problem will probably be too difficult for you to deal with alone. If you think you suffer from a lesser degree of social anxiety and that you can deal with it by yourself or mainly by yourself, there are several techniques you can use, which we will discuss in Chapters 4 and 5.

If you suffer from any degree of social anxiety, do you feel it has affected your life? If your answer is yes, in what ways do you feel that social anxiety has affected your life? What steps are you going to take to deal with the problem? Do you feel that your struggle with social anxiety has given you special insight that those who have not dealt with it lack? If you do, you're probably right!

3 SOCIAL ANXIETY, SELF-ESTEEM AND STRESS

If you have social anxiety, you probably already know that it can adversely affect your self-esteem and create intense stress. You have probably learned this from situations where you felt too intimidated to enter a social gathering and went home, and then felt guilty and silly afterwards. You might have also had an experience where you did not fully contribute and show your abilities during a work meeting simply because your social anxiety hindered you from doing so. It is easy to imagine how much stress and adverse effect on your self-esteem this could cause.

Unfortunately, the ability of social anxiety to cause stress and create self-esteem problems, and social anxiety and stress worsening the social anxiety, can constitute a vicious cycle that can be very difficult to break out of. Fortunately, however, if you are an introvert like us (which you probably are if you have social anxiety), you are at an advantage in dealing with your social anxiety! This is because we introverts have a high level of self-awareness. We have strong abilities with regard to being aware of our own thoughts and feelings. We have awareness of how those thoughts and feelings affect us. We also tend to have a high level of awareness of our motivations, or can easily develop this level of awareness. All of this is possible because of our strong capacity for introspection and reflection.

In order to help you realize how confident and stress-free you really deserve to be, we will discuss several additional introvert strengths! By the end of this list, you will realize how lucky you are to be an introvert!

1. Introspective ability and self-awareness

We have a profound ability to think about and understand our own feelings and motivations. We have an incredible capacity for reflection.

2. We are deep thinkers, and usually very creative.

You probably know that you have the ability to think deeply and consistently on any given topic or thought. You are able to easily understand complex concepts, and to think in a philosophical, eminently logical way.

3. We have strong focus.
People are often amazed by your ability to maintain focus. This makes you very good at seeing out long projects and other endeavors to their conclusion. Not only do you stick with them, you also enjoy doing so.

4. We have an independent spirit.
We are not afraid to live life on our own terms. We are able to easily think outside of the box in a big way! This gives us the potential to be especially creative, unique people! We tend to stand out in a crowd.

5. We are less impulsive, and tend to think things through properly.
We have excellent judgment, and are often wise beyond our years. This gives us great leadership potential.

6. We have much more of a capacity for being a visionary!
As we have strong introspection and deep thinking abilities, it is much more likely for us to have potential as visionaries.

7. We like to take part in meaningful, deep conversations.
We much prefer deep, fascinating conversation to meaningless small talk.

8. We are better at influence and persuasion than you think.
We tend to persuade and influence in a quiet, but highly effective manner.

9. We are excellent listeners and observers.
We are often noted for our keen abilities of listening and observation.

10. We are usually excellent with written, detailed communication.
You should probably try your hand at writing, as we often have great potential for this art.

You are probably asking, how exactly do I put to this to work in my struggle with the social anxiety/stress and self-esteem cycle? Don't worry, as we will show you how. By the end of the next few chapters, you will be well-equipped to succeed in this journey.

As we are introverts and enjoy spending time by ourselves just thinking, use some of that time to reflect on your strengths and to build your confidence. Learn to be kind to yourself in your thinking. Develop strategies for dealing with the obstacles you might face. If you are like us, you probably find it helpful to write things down. If this is the case, go ahead and do this. Keep a journal or notebook in which you write down positive things about yourself, and the ways in which your personality benefits you and makes you the great human being that you are!

Use your introspective skills to reflect your past and present experiences of stress and self-esteem. Has social anxiety affected your stress and self-esteem? If so, in what ways has it done so? How clearly did you recognize this effect at the time, or soon after that time? Take time to deeply reflect on these questions.

Self-awareness will help you to stay aware of your thoughts and your motivations, and make it much more likely for you to break free of the cycle of social anxiety, low self-esteem, and stress.

Once you have thought upon this subject, you will very likely want to learn about strategies and other techniques you can use to overcome the stress and negative self-esteem effects of social anxiety. Keep on reading to do exactly that. Find out what you need to do to take control of social anxiety's effects on your life!

PART II:
OVERCOMING SOCIAL ANXIETY AND SHYNESS

LISA KIMBERLY

4 OVERCOMING THE STRESS OF SOCIAL ANXIETY

We've learned that social anxiety and its effects can create stress in many different ways. Now we are going to learn about ways through which you can counteract the effects of social anxiety in this area. By the end of the chapter, you will have the tools you need to successfully address social anxiety stress!

1. Exercise more frequently.

You're probably asking, what on earth does exercise have to do with stress? What does it have to do with the stress I feel as a result of social anxiety? Well, the answer is that exercise helps with any kind of stress. It will assist you in thinking more clearly and objectively, and in being easier on yourself. As you might know, exercise encourages the release of special brain chemicals that make you have a better and more optimistic mood, and can help with confidence. Even just making sure to go for a short walk each day will help in this matter. It will benefit you to gradually increase your time spent exercising daily, as well.

2. Give yourself time to think and reflect, and challenge negative thoughts.

Our strength in the area of introspection and self-awareness make you a perfect candidate for using reflection in your quest of overcoming the stress of social anxiety. Take time to relax and simply think about the universe. Be kind to yourself. You need to realize that you have no control over many things that happen in life that are external to you, but that you do have the ability to control your thoughts and beliefs. Avoid living in the past or the future. Rather, focus the most on enjoying the present moment. When you have negative thoughts, always challenge them!

3. Think about and solidify your goals.

It can be very helpful to concretely think about and solidify your goals with regard to beating your social anxiety. One great way of doing this is to write your goals down! This is an activity that will appeal to, and help, and introverts like us the most. You will probably enjoy it. Get a special notebook for this purpose. Keep it in a special, but accessible place. You could even get a little notebook that you can carry around from place to place, for a sense of security in your journey. Make sure to keep a journal, too. In this, you can record the progress you make every day in getting closer and closer to achieving your goals.

4. Start small

Start out by taking small steps in your quest of overcoming your social anxiety. This can include small social risks. It can also involve altering seemingly minor habits of thinking. Give yourself credit for your accomplishments. Make sure to keep working on making them more and more significant and challenging. Examples of small social risks you could take include: making eye contact and smiling at a stranger, making a friendly comment to someone at a party (for instance, on how many people are there), and taking part in public speaking.

5. Practice makes perfect.

Don't be too hard on yourself! Remember like with so many other things in life, practice makes perfect in the area of social confidence. If you fail the first time you try to do something, try, try, and try again! You will find that the other techniques we discuss here will help you in this journey.

6. Find a more social hobby.

What are your current favorite hobbies? Do they require you to spend time with other people, or are they hobbies that really mainly favor solitude? Is there any way you could adjust your hobbies to make them include other people? If your favorite hobby is, for example, stamp collecting, maybe you could put together a stamp collecting enthusiast group. Or maybe you could join an existing one. Or if your favorite hobby is reading, join or put together a reading club that will meet, for instance, once a week, or once every couple of weeks. During those meetings, you can discuss your enjoyment and interpretations of the book in question. Maybe you could even bring in some books on social anxiety. Talk about "killing two birds with one stone"!

7. Learn about body language and facial expressions.

Most people do not realize how incredibly important body language and facial expressions are in human communication. The fact of the matter is that body language and facial expressions comprise a huge element in the ability of human beings to communicate with one another, and in how an individual's communications are interpreted. Take time to examine your own body language, and think about your own facial expressions. Look for other books and more information online specifically on the topic of non-verbal communication. Think about questions such as, how often do you make eye contact? Could you make eye contact more often? Does your body stance and facial expression make you seem closed off and unapproachable? What could you do to remedy this?

8. Understand and learn to control your body's responses.

How do you feel before a social event? Do you have a racing heartbeat? What about fast, shallow breathing? Do your hands feel clammy, and do you perspire more heavily? If you do have these responses, be kind to yourself. Realize that these are natural responses that human beings have when they are navigating an unknown situation. Simply focus on controlling them. If you focus on controlling your responses instead of thinking there is something wrong with you for having them in the first place, you are well on your way!

9. Find a cause you believe in and want to work for.

Finding a cause that you believe in and want to work for will likely help you forget about and overcome your social anxiety! Here is an example of this at work. Someone might feel passionately that something must be done to save a certain wildlife species. That person might join a group of people who feel the same way, and will work with these people to try to achieve a common goal. In this process, social anxiety is very likely to be put aside much more easily. And then, in working with these people, habits of confidence and ease in social situations will be formed.

10. Focus on the other person.

When you feel anxious while conversing with someone, try to focus completely on the other person and on what they are saying. This is likely to help reduce your level of self-conscientiousness. This, in turn, will lessen the effects of your social anxiety. As you practice getting more and more experience in having conversations with people, especially with strangers or people you only know as acquaintances, you will find yourself getting better and better at the process! Remember to always make eye contact with the person you are conversing with. Consciously think about and focus on what the person is saying, what the person is feeling, and the totality of what the person is saying. Look at their facial expressions, but do not let yourself jump to any negative conclusions in that regard! Keep your thinking objective.

11. Use breathing and muscle relaxation exercises.

A great way to deal with the stress of social anxiety is to use calming breathing exercises. These are especially helpful in the time just before a social situation, when you are getting the symptoms of shallow and quick breathing and accelerated heart rate. There is a great wealth of information on the wide variety of different breathing and muscle relaxation techniques online. One breathing and muscle relaxation technique that you probably didn't realize was one, is guided visualization. Of course, this is not only a breathing and muscle relaxation technique, but also a psychological one. In order to do guided visualization, you need to focus on positive, happy images. These will counteract or block out your negative thoughts. While you are focusing on the positive, happy images, you must breathe mindfully and deeply.

5 IMPROVING YOUR SELF-ESTEEM

If you have social anxiety, you are probably already very aware that this anxiety can have a major effect on your self-esteem. Low self-esteem can make your social anxiety worse. It can be a vicious cycle, but by the end of this chapter, you will have learned invaluable ways of improving your self-esteem! You're a great person, and you deserve to have great self-esteem.

But where to start? Improving your self-esteem in the face of social anxiety may seem like an insurmountable task. Don't let yourself think that way! It is not insurmountable.

1. Challenge negative thoughts, and refuse to be hard on yourself.

One of the most important things you must do in order to improve your self-esteem is to challenge negative thoughts. This means whenever you have a negative thought about yourself and your worth as a person, you must immediately challenge it. You must show yourself that it is unfair and irrational.

2. Learn to recognize your abilities and positive attributes.

Depending on how long you have had social anxiety, your self-esteem might be battered to the extent where you have forgotten about the wide array of abilities and positive attributes that belong to you! Work hard to remember and recognize everything that is wonderful about you. It can be very helpful to keep a little notebook or journal where you record everything you are good at, and everything you accomplish! This will help to solidify these positive thoughts in your brain. It can help to remind you of your strengths when you are going through a rough patch.

3. Recognize your introversion as a strength!

If you have social anxiety, there is a good chance that you are an introvert. If this is the case, you will already know that we introverts typically go through a lot in Western society! Introversion is generally regarded as undesirable. Often, it is assumed that the world should belong to extroverts. The truth, though, is that we have an amazingly wide array of strengths! You will remember that we discussed those strengths earlier on in this book. We want to make you aware that our strengths will actually make your goal of improving your self-esteem in the face of social anxiety an easier process! This is mainly because of our abilities in the areas of introspection and self-awareness.

4. Recognize the reality of your social anxiety.

If you have social anxiety, embarrassment about the problem might have led to your denying its existence, to others and even to yourself. The fact of the matter is that you have absolutely nothing to feel embarrassed about! You have nothing to be ashamed about! Having social anxiety does not mean that we are weak, or weird, or useless. The fact that we have social anxiety only means that we are very sensitive people, and that we have obstacles to overcome. Luckily, we are wonderfully strong and resilient people!

5. Be kind to yourself while going through the process of reducing your social anxiety.

Don't be impatient with yourself! Be a kind and respectful teacher. Give yourself whatever time you need to reduce your social anxiety, and to improve your self-esteem. Neither of these things will happen overnight. They are not expected to do so! Unrealistic expectations will set you up for disappointment. There will probably be times when you go a few steps backwards in your progress. Don't despair! You will move forward. You will achieve your goals. You are on the path, and staying on it is all that matters! The time it will take you to get to the ultimate destination is nowhere near as important as that!

6. Be aware of the potential benefits of Cognitive Behavioral Therapy.

Have you ever heard of Cognitive Behavioral Therapy? It is a technique used by psychologists, therapists, and other mental health professionals to gradually change your thinking, and ultimately the wiring of your brain through behavior and cognition. The key with Cognitive Behavioral Therapy is consistently building upon accomplishments. If you have social anxiety and low self-esteem, Cognitive Behavioral Therapy might be very helpful for you in your journey.

7. Get to know other people who are struggling with social anxiety.

Getting to know other people who have social anxiety will give you a greater sense of perspective on your problem. It will help and support you in your journey, and give you more practice in social interaction. You will have a greater sense of community. Perhaps you can find a social anxiety support group!

6 TAKING CHARGE OF YOUR LIFE

Social anxiety can pose some of its greatest difficulties in the area of daily life, including friendships, relationships, and your career. You may have felt these effects yourself. You may be suffering in various different ways as a result. Don't worry! By the end of this chapter, you will know how you can lessen the effects that social anxiety has on your life. You will know how to make sure that you reach your real potential!

The most important thing to remember here is the importance of starting small. Starting small is smart because it will ensure you will not feel overwhelmed and possibly give up. Also, it will give you a regular source of a sense of accomplishment. Each small step will lead to another one, and before you know it all of your small steps and accomplishments will have added up to something much larger. You will have meaningful control over your life!

Lessening Social Anxiety's Effects on Your Daily Life

Of course, the first step you must take is to follow the advice we provided in previous chapters in order to lessen the social anxiety itself. But what should you do in the meantime, while you are in the process of addressing the social anxiety, but it is still a major factor in your life? What should you do if you find that you in fact have social anxiety so severe as to require the assistance of a mental health professional? Surely we all have the right to a fulfilled and productive life! Below are suggestions that will help you ensure that social anxiety has the mildest effect on your life possible.

1. Stay aware.
Be kind to yourself. Stay aware of the reality of your social anxiety, and

give yourself credit for having the courage to address it. It is important that we never underestimate this! Giving ourselves proper credit and acknowledging our courage and determination will give us extra confidence. This boosted confidence will aid us in daily life.

2. Keep a journal.

Keep a journal of the courage and diligence you have shown in your quest to lessen the effects of your social anxiety on your daily life. Keeping this record and referring to it when we have a moment of doubt will help increase our confidence in our daily lives.

3. Use your strengths.

You are an amazing person with lots of strengths. It's about time that you recognized that. Use this acknowledgement to help build your confidence! And devote time to developing and building upon your many strengths.

4. Open up.

Do the people in your life know about your social anxiety? Do they recognize its reality and validity? Make sure that people know about your social anxiety. If they know little about it or dismiss it, educate them. Don't be afraid to assert yourself. You deserve it.

5. Respect your boundaries.

As we go through the process of addressing our social anxiety, we will go through different stages at which our boundaries are at different places. There is nothing wrong with this! Something that would be too much for you to do after one month of your journey, might be easy after one year, and so on. While you need to build on your small steps and challenge yourself to take social risks, stay aware on where you are and what you should do at a given point in time.

Reaching Your Potential

1. Let your light shine!

None of us wants to be seen as a braggart, or to be thought arrogant. However, people with social anxiety (and especially introverts like us) tend to "overdo" their humility. Something that a person with excellent confidence and no social anxiety would not think is boasting at all might seem like it to us. Don't fall into this trap! If you have an accomplishment, why shouldn't you take credit for it? Why shouldn't you get the recognition you deserve?

2. Develop your talents.

Recognize what your talents are, and do everything you can to develop them. Perhaps there is something you have always suspected you would be good at, but didn't have the confidence to approach. If there is, do something about it now!

3. Know that your contribution matters!

Your contribution is as least as important as, and perhaps even more important than, another person's. We have the right to have our opinions and ideas heard. This is especially important in the workplace. Meetings are a good example of when this practice is most relevant.

4. Assert yourself.

If you tend to be seen as a timid doormat by others, start making a change in this area! Make sure to learn to assert yourself whenever needed. If you have trouble developing this skill, there are a wide variety of assertiveness training books and courses out there. The idea of being assertive might seem a bit intimidating to you right now, but don't lose faith in yourself. You can do it!

5. Don't be overwhelmed by extroverts.

If you are an introvert like we are, you probably already know that feeling overwhelmed by extroverts is a very common occurrence. Extroverts, especially those who are more extremely extroverted, sometimes perceive us as people who they can talk over. Sometimes they even see us as people they can boss around. Assertiveness is especially crucial in this area. If you have this problem with extroverts, you need to be assertive and take a stand.

PART III:
SUCCEEDING AS AN INTROVERT

LISA KIMBERLY

7 BEING AN INTROVERT IN AN EXTROVERTED WORLD

If you live in a Western country, and especially in North America, it is unlikely you've ever doubted the fact that we live in a world that strongly favors extroversion. Sometimes it seems like extroverts are absolutely everywhere, and introverts nowhere to be seen. This is often the case when you turn on the television or watch a movie. Western cultures favors extroversion so much, in fact, that introversion is plagued with a number of unfair stereotypes. Let's go through some of them. After all, you have to know what you're fighting if you're going to win!

10 Introvert Myths

1. We just don't like being social.
According to this myth, we simply have no enjoyment in being around other people, and always want to be by themselves. We know that this is nonsense. We take as much enjoyment in being social as anyone else, as long as we are able to fulfill our need to have enough emotional recharging time. Just because we don't always enjoy being social on the extrovert's terms, doesn't mean that we don't like being social! Unfortunately, this myth sometimes results in us being excluded from invitations and activities.

2. We are boring.
We are anything but boring! We have vibrant inner lives, and when people get to know us, they are rewarded with being around our wonderful and fascinating personalities and intellects. Many extroverts don't seem to

want to make the effort to get to know us. They obviously don't realize how much they're missing out on!

3. We have nothing interesting to say.

Nonsense! We have an incredible amount of fascinating things to say. We are often wise beyond our years, and full of innovative and interesting ideas and opinions. We are often intellectual and have complex thinking skills. There are few people who can out-debate us when we get started!

4. We are incapable of succeeding in an extrovert-dominated profession.

This is absolutely untrue. We can succeed, as long as we make sure to have the right tools. This book is giving you the right tools right now! You're well on your way. Learn to assert yourself! Don't let yourself be pushed to the margins.

5. We don't have social skills.

This is yet another ridiculous myth. There is nothing about introversion that means that someone doesn't have social skills. We simply need time by ourselves to recharge. Just because we don't want to be in social situations 24/7 doesn't mean we don't know how to successfully do so.

6. We don't know how to have fun and enjoy themselves.

This is another silly stereotype that you have probably come across time and time again. You know that we know how to enjoy ourselves! Who cares if extroverts don't realize that? It's their loss. When we are with people we know well and with whom we feel comfortable with, we can be the most fun-loving people on the planet. Lots of us have amazing senses of humor.

7. We need to become extroverts.

Here's the big one! Yes, extroverts by and large seem to think that their way to be is the only way to be, and that we have to follow their lead. They're wrong! We're sure this isn't any great surprise. Unfortunately, many introverts feel very strong pressure to be extroverted all the time. Trying to fulfill this expectation can cause a lot of emotional stress, and even emotional burnout.

8. Extroversion is "normal", while introversion isn't.

Closely related to the myth above, is the popular idea that to be extroverted is to be normal, while to be introverted is to be lacking in normality. This has mainly been caused by the fact that extroverts outnumber introverts substantially.

9. We aren't happy.

Isn't this a silly idea? Unfortunately, there are many extroverts who always seem to assume we feel sad, or are generally not very happy. We introverts can have feelings of happiness more intense than those of others but not show it as obviously. We don't always feel the need to externally show our happiness. There's nothing wrong with this!

10. We lack ambition.

There is no doubt that this is one of the most illogical and unfair introvert myths. Introverts are often among the most intensely ambitious people in the world. This is partly due to our incredible capacity for focus and introspection.

As inaccurate and unfair as these stereotypes are, we think we can all agree that they are prevalent in Western culture (especially in North America). They need to be done away with, but until then what are we introverts to do? We find ourselves constantly coming up against labels that can hold us back—but only if we let them! We can overcome them.

The first thing you need to do is take control of our own self-image. See yourself through your own eyes, through an objective lens, rather than through the prejudiced ones of others. Be aware of the myths about introverts that are out there, and realize that every one of them is nonsense. They have nothing to do with you! They have nothing to do with who you are. If other people believe these stereotypes, that is their choice, and their problem. Refuse to make it yours!

Don't accept the labels that others seek to impose on you. Don't let anyone impose labels on you, and box you in. Don't let your life be defined and molded by what others think that you can and can't do.

8 BUILDING CONFIDENCE

Like most of us, you probably know how very important confidence is in daily life. Confidence affects everything, from what choices we make to what impression we give of ourselves to others. Confidence affects our self-esteem.

In this chapter, you will learn what you need to know about confidence, and about steps you can and should take to improve your confidence.

An important step in the journey to better self-confidence is taking stock of and acknowledging our strengths. You probably remember that in chapter 3 we read a list of advantages and strengths we introverts possess and can benefit from. Just so you don't have to turn back to that chapter, here is a recap of that list:

1. Introspective ability and self-awareness
2. We are deep thinkers, and probably very creative.
3. We have strong focus.
4. We have an independent spirit.
5. We are less impulsive, and tend to think things through properly.
6. We have much more of a capacity for being a visionary!
7. We like to take part in meaningful, deep conversations.
8. We are better at influence and persuasion than you think.
9. We are excellent listeners and observers.
10. We are usually excellent with written, detailed communication.

How many of these strengths do you recognize in yourself? Remember that if you confidence level is not currently the greatest, you might not recognize some that you actually do in reality possess. What other strengths do you have? What things are you good at? You owe it to yourself to recognize your strengths. You owe it to yourself to develop and take advantage of them to the greatest extent possible.

One of the topics we are going to focus on in this chapter is how you should and can develop your strengths, to build up your confidence. We also discuss confidence building generally, and the importance of awareness of the "shy and quiet" label trap. We are pretty sure you have come across that trap a number of times, like most of us introverts!

An important thing to remember is that, contrary to the stereotypes, we introverts are not intrinsically low in confidence. We are not born that way. It is the fact that we tend to be ostracized that affects our confidence, from year to year. All the factors come together into a vicious cycle, but it's a cycle out of which you can break!

Do you have low self-confidence? Here is a basic test, to give you a general idea of whether or not you have a self-confidence problem. But remember, whatever result you get, keep reading this chapter! There is no one in the world that has absolutely perfect self-confidence, and we can always improve! The information in this chapter and in this book will help you do so.

Confidence Test

1. Usually, how willing are you to take a stand that some others won't approve of, because you feel it's right?
a) Very often
b) Sometimes
c) Rarely

2. How willing are you to take well thought out risks, that you feel could bring you real rewards?
a) Very willing
b) Somewhat willing
c) Not willing

3. When you make a mistake, what is your most likely reaction?
a) I will admit it and learn from it.
b) I might admit to it. I'll likely learn from it.
c) I'll do everything possible to cover it up, and/or I'll be in denial.

4. Do you ever catch yourself blatantly boasting about your accomplishments?
a) No. I am proud of my accomplishments, but I never feel the need to boast.
b) If I do, it's very rare.
c) Yes, sometimes I feel I need to do so, to make myself feel better

about myself.

5. What is your usual response when people compliment you?
a) I graciously accept the compliment.
b) I might be a little hesitant to accept it, but I usually do.
c) I usually protest, and discount the compliment in some way.

For each a) answer, give yourself 3 points. For each b) answer, give yourself 2 points. For each c) answer, give yourself 1 point.

SCORING

11 to 15 points: You have a strong confidence level.
6-10: Your confidence level is generally good, but there is a significant amount of room for growth.
0-5: Your confidence level is currently low.
Now that you have a good, general idea of what your confidence level probably is, it's time to think about setting goals.

Setting Goals

Setting and achieving goals is of huge importance in the confidence building process. Remember, though, what we said earlier about "starting small". Achieving goals and confidence building will not necessarily happen overnight. However, if you start small in your goal setting, you will arrive at achievements more quickly. You will build up your confidence step by step.

You're probably asking what sort of goals we are talking about. What sorts of goals should you set, in order to aid in your confidence building?

You should focus on developing your abilities and strengths. Doing this will not only give you a sense of accomplishment. It will also help you to see how meaningful and useful your strengths actually are. Both of these factors will be crucial in the growth and improvement of your self-confidence.

Remember the list of the typical strengths of introverts that we gave you. If you are an introvert, chances are very good that you have several, if not all, of these incredible strengths! Recognize this, and focus on developing them. Start small, and think of small ways you can validate each of these strengths in your mind, and to further develop them in different ways. Build upon your small steps as you go!

Monitor Your Thinking

Stay aware of your thinking, and challenge any negative thoughts that creep into your head. How do you challenge them? You challenge them through using reason and fairness! Be a true and kind friend to yourself. That is definitely something that you deserve!

The "Shy and Quiet" Label

You may find that one of the biggest obstacles in the confidence building process is the "shy and quiet" label that others have imposed on you. For example, you could find this a bit intimidating when you are trying to make a point of speaking out more often. Don't let this intimidate you! See yourself through your own eyes, not through those of others.

Something else to remember is that just because someone is shy and quiet some of the time, doesn't mean that they are all of the time! If you feel shy or quiet at any given time, there's nothing wrong with that. That doesn't give others the right to label and limit you!

9 INTROVERTS IN THE WORKPLACE

As an introvert, you have probably come across a number of challenges in the workplace. However, don't make the mistake of thinking these challenges came about as a result of there being something "wrong" with your introversion. On the contrary, most often problems arise as a result of the biases and stereotypes held by others. If you are in a profession that is dominated primarily by extroverts, you will have an especially good idea of what we're talking about. Chances are good that you have been pressured to dismiss your strengths as an introvert. You have likely been pressured to do everything in your power to become an extrovert, probably experiencing burn-out and exhaustion in the process.

The fact of the matter, however, is that we can succeed in absolutely any career. Don't by any means feel that there are only a certain number of jobs that you can do well in. Your strengths as an introvert make you an incredible workplace asset! Focus on your wide array of strengths.

Our Written Communication Skills are Incredible.

Don't underestimate the potential you have in the area of written communication. If you do not already feel you write well, work on developing this skill. As an introvert, chances are excellent that you have the intrinsic potential to be a formidably great written communicator. These skills are vital and indispensable in any workplace. They are necessary and valued in pretty much every field. Their value is not limited to fields that we generally associate with writing, not by any means. But if you have not yet chosen a career, or you are thinking about a career change for any reason, maybe you should consider a field that has an especially strong writing focus.

We Are Wonderfully Creative.

We are great at coming up with innovative and exciting ideas! You've probably heard people talk about the importance of being able to think "outside of the box" with regard to jobs, and in preparation for job interviews. Well, introverts are usually much better at thinking outside of the box and coming up with truly original ideas than extroverts are.

Our creative abilities make us assets in any career field! But if you have not yet chosen a career, or if for any reason you are thinking about a career change, maybe think about taking into account your creative abilities in your decision-making process. There are many career fields out there that put special focus on creativity.

We Have Sound Judgment.

Our introverted tendency to think things out properly before speaking or acting makes us have much better judgment and ability to act wisely than typically possessed by extroverts. This tendency towards sound judgment gives us strong leadership potential. We are good at focusing on and appraising different options, and taking the time to think thoroughly on what the best options are. This is an ability of which many extroverts would be envious.

Our Listening Skills are Enviable.

We introverts have wonderful listening skills. We are generally known for this, and you should definitely devote some time to developing your listening skills to the best of your ability. Your listening skills make you an invaluable workplace team member. In workplace meetings, maybe try to find ways to demonstrate and call attention to your listening skills. If you hear one of your co-workers present an interesting idea, maybe tell them what your understanding of the idea is, and what your opinion of it is. This will help to show people that while they may think you are just avoiding talking, you are actually listening intently and at an advanced level.

Our Focus is Formidable.

We introverts have an excellent ability to focus. Our focus is generally much better than that of the average extrovert. This ability is invaluable in the workplace. This is especially the case with regard to special and vital projects and incentives. You are trustworthy and dependable. Your ability to keenly and consistently focus contributes greatly to your potential as a leader.

You Are An Amazing Researcher.

Your focus and deep thinking abilities make you a great researcher. Many career fields make use of this ability. Try to think about the ways you could apply it in your own field. Or, if you have not yet chosen a career, maybe think about careers where you could put this skill to special use.

You Work Independently Excellently.
You have an extremely strong ability to work independently with very little direction. We tend to be much better at this than extroverts. This skill adds to your general dependability.

We Are Great Leaders!
As a result of all of our incredible workplace strengths, experts have finally begun to clue in to the fact that our presence is absolutely crucial to a successful workplace. It is acknowledged that a good balance of introverts and extroverts are needed. It is also acknowledged that introverts actually tend to be wonderful leaders. The four skill areas we just discussed come together to make us strong in the area of leadership. Awareness of this fact is becoming more and more prevalent.

As it is so clear that introverts are a workplace asset in many different ways, you may be wondering why it is that there are so many misconceptions out there. The fact is that many stereotypes favoring extroverts in the workplace come from general cultural misconceptions. They also specifically come from portrayals of the workplace put forward in movies and television shows, and popular culture in general. Don't let all of this nonsense bring you down! Focus on and develop your abilities, and let your light shine to its fullest extent! Don't let anyone bring you down.

10 INTROVERT ICONS

Well, we've certainly covered a lot in this book! You have learned about your emotions and experiences. You have learned about what an incredible, talented person you are, and how much potential you really have. On top of all of that, you have gained tools and methods of thinking that will help you reach your greatest potential! Chances are good that you have gained new hope and optimism.

When you reach your potential and show the world your talents, you will certainly not be alone! There have been and are a great many incredibly gifted introverts in our world. Let's talk about some of them!

Bill Gates

As he is arguably the most famous person in the world, you probably don't need to be told that Bill Gates is a co-founder of Microsoft, and is the richest man in the world. He has done a large amount of philanthropy, mainly through the Bill and Melinda Gates Foundation.

Bill Gates is well-known as one of the world's most famous and successful introverts. He has made it clear that he is proud of his introversion, and does not try to hide it in any way. He knows that his strengths as an introvert have helped make him who he is! He has specifically made reference to the introverted ability to have great focus.

J.K. Rowling

As J.K. Rowling is the author of the *Harry Potter* book series, you have probably heard of her on more than a few occasions! J.K. Rowling wrote her incredible books and achieved her success under very difficult economic circumstances. It wasn't a fast process, but her focus allowed her to finally prevail.

J.K. Rowling credits her ability to think up such original and imaginative ideas, and to focus for long and extended periods of time in difficult circumstances, to her introversion.

Albert Einstein
Without doubt, you already know that Albert Einstein is generally considered the greatest genius to have ever existed. The strongly introverted qualities that Einstein possessed seem generally common to many famous geniuses. Albert Einstein's introverted ability for incredible focus and deep, extensive thought processes helped to make this astonishing accomplishments possible.

Warren Buffett
Warren Buffett is one of the world's greatest and most famous business entrepreneurs and investors. He has referred to himself as an introvert, and has attributed some of his success to his introverted characteristics of careful thought and sound, measured judgment.

Emma Watson
Being an actress and model does not mean you must be an extrovert! Emma Watson has said herself that she is an introvert, and a proud one at that. Although she is perfectly comfortable with being an introvert now, though, at first she worried that there was something wrong with her. She gradually came to understand that being an introvert is something of which she should be proud!

Steven Spielberg
The movie director Steven Spielberg is yet another highly successful and creative introvert. He has spoken about his introversion, and said one of his favorite things to do is having a movie watching marathon all by himself! Like many introverted creative people, Steven Spielberg uses his art as a form of self-expression.

Audrey Hepburn
The legendary classic actress Audrey Hepburn is another famous and highly accomplished introvert. Audrey Hepburn recognized herself as an introvert, and talked about how difficult it was for her to be extroverted, at times of her life when she felt obliged to do so. She was a very introspective person, and loved simple contemplation.

Marissa Mayer
Marissa Mayer is the current CEO and president of Yahoo. She has been ranked as the world's 16th most powerful businesswoman. Marissa Mayer has stated that she is an introvert, and is shy. She has also said that her decision to work in a field she has real passion for has made everything

she does, even things that are outside of her comfort zone, easy! A good tip for everyone! Her insight is typical of an introvert.

Wendy Kopp

Wendy Kopp is the founder and Chair of the Board of the non-profit organization, Teach for America (TFA). Its goal is to place teachers with strong educational accomplishments, in less privileged schools. Wendy Kopp has stated that she is an introvert and is shy, and that some of the things she has to do for her position do not come easily. But the passion she feels for her cause and her organization, and her introvert's focus and deep thinking ability moves her forward.

Keanu Reeves

Keanu Reeves, a very prominent actor, is a self-professed introvert. In fact, he is extremely well-known for being an introvert in Hollywood. He is extremely focused and determined, both common characteristics of introverts. He is known for being an extraordinary work ethic on set.

We think it can't be denied that this is a list of distinguished, fascinating, and successful people. And all of these people are or were proud introverts! They all used and developed their many strengths and achieved great success, just as we are certain you will now!

CONCLUSION

My greatest desire is for this book to fill you with hope.

To give you that feeling that you can change your destiny.

If you have that one feeling then I know I have succeeded with this book.

You are in charge of your destiny.

There is nothing wrong with being introverted.

Twenty-five percent of the population is introverted.

It that was a disease then we could say the same thing about being left-handed.

Only ten percent of people are left handed.

You can use the exercises from this book to build up your self-confidence and overcome your social anxiety when you need to.

You don't have to become an extrovert and completely change your personality.

But now you have the tools to overcome your fears and to start living the life you have always dreamed of.

There is nothing that can stop you now!

ABOUT THE AUTHOR

Lisa Kimberly is a woman who is trying to heal the world one book at a time. She loves helping people and sharing her personal struggles and stories of triumph. She is so grateful that you took the time to read her book and can't wait to hear about your success overcoming social anxiety.

Website
http://www.lisakimberly.com

CPSIA information can be obtained
at www.ICGtesting.com
Printed in the USA
LVOW04s1118211116
513901LV00010B/171/P